You Are Better Than My Pen

Selected Poems
by Mike Jenkins

ISBN: 9-798874-315962

https://michaeljenkins.co.uk

Published by HyperPress (Brighton)
https://chrismiddleton.company
through Kindle Direct Publishing (KDP).

Edited, designed and illustrated by Chris Middleton.

Mike Jenkins

Mike is a poet, storyteller, and actor, trained at London's Guildhall School of Music & Drama. He has written three plays for the stage – directing two of them in London and Chichester – and is a founding member and co-host of the popular Chichester open-mic night, Words Out Loud. Since 2023, he has also hosted their entertainment evening, Seven Up.

This is his first full poetry collection.

You Are Better Than My Pen

Selected Poems
by Mike Jenkins

My Boyfriend is a Poet

My boyfriend is a poet, don't you know?

He reels off Haiku
when he pauses by the bed
lit by light of dawn.

He makes a thousand drifting summers' days
They are more lovely and more temperate
Than the darling of the lord of ways
To raise the sea to sky with fleet of foot
And smudge the grey to Saturday so bright
In dazzle innocence he does this much;
Ignite the morn, the noon and anguished night
Lo! Winter's bite shall not escape his touch
Full curled like whisky heat among the chill
He wanders with me, hand around my cloud
Of shifting, dawning, lowing, longing still
I rise again astounded from this shroud.
> So long as I do breathe and walk my way
> So long lives this in awe of words to say.

And so, he writes with eyes azure
with kindness that could detonate a
dozen armies of scribbling academics
and scatters stanzas of astonishing resilience
at the slings and arrows of life's
downright outrageous calamities.

And to
topple it all
with a flash of his smile
pens a cinquain all the while
there's wine

Splashing
with love heartfelt
round the rhyme holding time
Taking his hand in mine we are
still here.

On the Steps of Heaven

We both knew
we'd never kiss like that again
on the steps of Heaven
If only we'd not drunk quite as much
and if only
mobile phones had been invented
or if only
I had carried a pen
in my top pocket

like I have ever since
that night.

Otherly Love
For Craig

Otherly and
southerly and
occasionally lovely
I cross the Atlantic Ocean
and worship a saint
in my shower.

He says he does
not perform miracles
But being otherly
I know otherwise.

I've seen the sun rise
in his eyes and
set soft below
the otherly skies and

Bless the others
in disguise
Gliding through the sea of streets
and sheets of greets and heats of meets
Graceful as a tea clipper
carrying a cargo of choirs in his heart
and a symphony in his skin.

Where to begin to convey
the miracle of the everyday?

Hidden in plain sight
in a hackney carriage
amid the night.

Like a jewel in a vast empty ocean
a haven for the traveller's plight
An isle for my otherly love
to rest from flight.

You Are Better Than My Pen

you look better than my pen does
in that bulky winter coat
you frown better than my pen does
in shirt sleeves
and ordinary coffee-coloured
cathedral leaves
and you do mystery,
camaraderie
and that friendly variety
of putting others before yourself
better than my pen does.
you move better than my pen does
you laugh better than my pen does
you ache better than pen does and you
break better than my pen does
(in private
out on the edges of my imagination
in the darkening shadows of a block-paved car park, perhaps)
you lift your heart into a smile better than my pen does
you breathe better than my pen does
you smoke better than my pen does and
you almost certainly taste, smell and feel better
than my pen does.
you just do
you
far better than my pen does
and yet still
in this still dance across the keyboard
when it's really, really
still
for now
it's as close
to you
as I can
get.

With Keats I Sit and Wait

Here
we sit together
the world moving around us
with an uncertain almost
astonished gait

here we sit on curve of
Eastgate Square and
wait

for that spark of unifying fire
that leaps from window ledge above
cradles child curling about your burnished leg
stops passers-by who may
in brackets wonder
(who is he?)
in stillness kept serene
what are those words about the curve?
what does it mean to dream
of high romance?

Ah… look
with eyes of heart and see him here
alive
in you
in me

Stay awhile and breathe to fill
in clouds and spires
in streets of moving

still.

Morning Bells

In a tiny Tuscan village
high up on a hill
I wake to the sound of church bells
sounding out a warning
saying somehow you are still
bewitched.

His name was Pablo
and he just walked out of a fresco
sat down and had coffee with me.
He told me about David and
Michelangelo and how together
they would overthrow the meaning of art.

Without even a backward glance
he stepped back into that fresco
remains there frozen in time and
somewhere in a notebook he is forever mine.

The bells rang out for longer that day
as if there was something else they wanted to say.

I sipped my coffee

astonished at the sweet
maddening
and bitter, lingering
taste of longing.

I Could Move Out West

I could move out West
and be a simple man
buttoned up in forgotten dreams
my heart chained beneath my vest
swallowing yearnings howling screams
get along as well as I can
rest backfooted in Sunday best
thank the Lord that I am blessed
with at least the devil I know
who sows fields of the unfinished
day after day into every vein
frozen in mid-air, a life fermented
in disappointment, boy demented
never meant it
to be this way.

I could move out West
failure heaving in my chest
eyes fixed groundward
hands full of rubble, build a nest
out of those broken years
that I keep stacked up in books.

But I won't.
I'll stay where I am
Somehow figure out a plan
to be a better man
the one that others see
glimpsed in the twinkling of a smile
now and then or the flick of a pen
across an empty page.

I won't go West then
I'll stay here
be the other Hamlet
the one who chose life, yes
I'll get dressed and
go dancing.

If you're passing
on your way out West,
don't pass.
Come and take me.

Falling

I am falling
and I know you thought you could catch me
but I'm not sure that you can
or maybe you thought you knew me
but perhaps you just knew the man
I could have been.
I am not that man
nor was meant to be
no
not some Prince Hamlet
nor Capulet either
no, no, no
I am not a pair of claws
or pre-prepared applause
ready to warm the room.
No
more likely a Bennett cliché
destined for the library
in a grey coat on an ordinary Tuesday
as invisible as the world's greatest literature
sitting silently on shelves
that no one visits.
I have not been opened
let alone read cover to cover
and what a terrible waste of
every word
every breath
every blush of blood in the veins
that has been written to my lover
the one who never came
the one who waited instead
in the distant dust
of another life.
Oh well.
The cafe on the front does a nice
egg and chips and
Susan
the women there
knows a broken heart when she sees one
patches them up with builders' tea.

Life isn't so bad
really.
I thought I saw you
the other day
but then you turned to look my way
and your wife and children
came sweeping under your arm
taking shelter there.
No
it was just my imagination
as ever
running away with me.
There's a pub round here
full of youth and life and future
I sit there sometimes
waiting for you
like a fool.
I am falling
so respectfully
I'm not sure you'll even notice
when I'm gone.

Dragging His Beat

It's become a little lazy
in the hazy fog of waiting
through the years now since the words starting marching
from the tip of his pen
they seem to say the same kind of thing
again and again
and lately there's a haltering faltering
sort of spluttering kind of groping
with a
dead
heart
stop
start
kind of
syncopated rhythm in the cloak-dark
soft-shoe scuffing park of dazzling stars
that have taken to wandering outside the gates
of heaven.
Each and every one of them
of course, of course,
has light spilling from his sneakers
and each one looks at me
with a weary understanding
that knows I've thrown myself under
his bus already.
Another one bites the murderous dancefloor
which of course is much stickier than before
and it's become much harder to wake from that dream.
it lingers and drags its fingers into the daylight beams
and the beat is in retreat
out of time it doesn't so much scream
as wail and whimper.
The summer is coming
and one wonders if this year
he'll finally stumble
tango rubble fumble to the ground
having been shot through the heart
with one hundred staccato rounds
from one of those angels
whose light spills out
from their sneakers.

The Unkempt Rose

There's a well-dressed thorn
on the ragged road tonight
ripping shirts off backs of children
who've haven't learned to fight
in quite
the right way
just yet.

But look a little closer
in the cracks of city wall
where there's an unkempt rose that
knows it doesn't know it all and
yet it knows that there's a code
in the roots of truth in mud
and its song of raging beauty
soaks the city thick with blood
of the beauty of the rose that is rose in name and form
as the city walls are crumbling and the light of dawn is rumbling
all those well-dressed thorns who forgot the love of earth
tear themselves from the garden and
who wither in the birth
of the unkempt rose
that refuses to grow
in rows
rising ragged and unruly
from the beauty
of the truly, deeply, muddy, messy throes
where his thorns are not concealed in the pretty awful clothes
of the dread-rode wolf or the lowly lamb
he is cutting through concrete singing the song *I am*
singing truth from mother earth
I am THAT
I am.

Saturday Men

Saturday men
wash cars and mow lawns
play football and cut down trees
build ponds and arse about in sheds
put up shelves and put down dust sheets
paint walls and water gardens.

Saturday men
go running in the park
tinker with the parts from engines long dead
meet up with mates down the boozer
and don't really ever talk
about how they feel.

Saturday men loom large around town
getting stuff done and getting down
to business.
They don't stand still for long
the moment you spot one
in the blink of an eye
(or before any kind of Freudian analysis has begun)
they're gone
shot off like a dart
to the hardware store to find that
part to replace the one
that broke.

Saturday men are just doing their thing
in a Saturday man kind of way
and I watch as they pass
like buses or trains
as they bustle and whistle away
back to the suburbs, behind lawns neatly kept
in a house stood sturdy and strong
and Saturday men don't really know
what it's like to not belong.

But it's not their fault
for being men
who were built for Saturday
and it's not my fault

for wanting one of them
to come and take me away
to a house in the smart part of town
behind lawns neatly kept
and pathways swept like clockwork
every Saturday.

Pretend Shopping

I enjoyed our day
pretending to go shopping together
as if we were…
together.

Neither you nor I
spoke of our play
but went along with it anyway
and seemed to find it comfortable
Picking out patio plants
side by side
trying on a potential life
to see which size would fit.

Me pushing the trolley, or you?
we tried both and did not decide
one way or the other.

I have no idea if we
looked the part
but I do know
I left as much of my heart
with you as I dared.

Not too much to frighten the birds
but enough perhaps to take root,
planted alongside the sunflowers
where I know you'll stand each day
to inspect progress.

I wonder if we'll ever try on some other scene?
Perhaps I could pretend to greet you
coming home from work?
Or we could bicker about the best
place to park the car?
Under the shade of the tree
or free from the threat of windfall?

In any case
after all that
I drove home alone

to my quiet, little flat
and wondered if you'd agree
with me
on the best spot for that patio plant?

We'll have to wait and see.

The Big Break

I was only 22 when I fell through
the rabbit hole
of collaptic synaptic
perception.
Iris Murdoch was staring out
at me from the front page of a Sunday newspaper
absent terror and confusion scribbled
across her face as she
lost her place
in a quaint Oxfordshire garden.

It was as if the chasm in me
was looking at the chasm in her
and round we went together
for 22 years
looking for the exit.

It was 1998
on the Archway road
where the windows in my bedroom
rattled as the No.43 bus
rumbled
on its way
to the belly of the city.

It was a pity really
the teachers would think
as they watched all that potential sink
into the blankness of a
a pause that would make even Pinter

uncomfortable.

The maverick Russian theatre director
looked clean into my eyes
in the basement canteen
and spoke in kind, fatherly tones

his translator Natasha
explaining "what Vasily mean"
is that even the subway
in London
breaks down
now and then.

Now and then
and now and then
went like that
Now and again.

And again
It's entirely dramatic of course
that. somehow, I have always felt
the pause never stopped.

That perhaps the pharmaceuticals
kept the whole show in unfinished suspension
where still
I am there
aged 22
out beyond belief
in a newspaper cutting
with Iris Murdoch
preserved and still

waiting for my big break.

Other Versions of People You Know

What does it mean
when you see a crow
on the path outside your door?

And what of seeing people you know
as they used to be
in your life before?

I saw my Dad yesterday
having lunch at an Italian restaurant.
He was 34, I'd say
and would have been working all day
in a factory or driving a truck.

Except it wasn't him
drinking white wine and eating calamari
on a Tuesday afternoon.
He doesn't go to Italian restaurants anyway
he drinks cans of Guinness
by the pond in his garden.
He's 76 now and kinder than he ever was
(if that's even possible).

And one summer, in a Market Town in Hampshire
I saw my best friend Peter
from school way back when.
He was older than then
in his 40s I reckon
drinking beer with friends in a pub.

Except it wasn't Peter
because his life
broke apart
after his wife
was taken by cancer
and his heart followed.

I saw my older sister last year
when she was so much younger
at the Asda buying oranges and tea.
She looked so much happier than then
and she also looked through me
as if we'd never met at all.

We had met, though
when we were small
and she was someone different
who didn't like oranges much and rarely went to Asda.
She liked Madonna and Wham and hung around with older boys

And that boy I fell in love with
at college
when I didn't know what it would mean
turned up not two weeks gone by
aged nineteen
on a dating app
would you believe
as gay as the day is long.

But no. That's not it at all
something's gone oddly wrong.
He lives with his missus, a wee girl and a springer spaniel
he works for the council
(long hours it seems)
I can't get him out for a pint
for all the plates in China.

What does it mean
when you see them so
wandering around your life like that
as free as spirits long dead?

I don't know, I don't know
but the crow keeps coming
to stand at my door
bold as an omen in a low budget flick
it crooks its head in quizzical fashion
as if to say: you really don't get it
do you?

I keep seeing other versions
of people I know
in the town where I live now.

If I could
I'd decipher the meaning
but really, in all honesty,
I don't know how.

The Reedless Hush

Along this canal
when I was a pale student
a friend saw a pike
leap up and out of the grey glassy water and
eat a stray duckling whole.

The pike was brown-green and nobbly
with crooked teeth and sickly eyes
the bright startled yellow of the chick's downy feathers
drowning in the gullet of the river monster
as it submerged to the silty depths of the canal
and the bright green reeds make a pact among themselves
never to tell.

Sometimes I feel like I am that duckling
swallowed whole by some ferocious beast and
sometimes I feel I am that villain
gobbling up the meek.

And sometimes
more often than I care to admit
I feel I am the deep,
the ever-flowing river
that swallows and holds it all
in the rippling belly of movement
towards the guts of the sea
emptying into the rush and mess
and the reedless hush
of infinity.

The Vow of Spring

I promised I would wait here for you
while the world was cold and sleeping
I've never been very far away
just hidden under your feet.

I've been watching you
through the Winter
that night you fell asleep crying
I planted a thousand crocus bulbs in St Matthews Park
and sprayed daffodils along the hedgerows.

And when your heart began to crack open
the day your Mother died
I prepared meadows scattered with wild
raucous flowers
and put an oak tree in the centre of each one.

I never go away.
I only wait
to rise again
and bring with me the colours
of your suffering
transfigured for the season.

There is a reason
the earth is round
and the sun and the moon are too
and a reason the ground is fertile
with other versions of you.

I found you again
like I do each year
I promised I wouldn't go far
so rejoice with the lamb, with the meadow in bloom
rejoice
for I am here.

Mother's Pride
For Mum, on Mother's Day, 27th March 2022

Liquified Sunday roast
in blinding June sunlight
we stood side by side.
After twelve hours on an operating table
I told you
they told me
I am not able to eat
solid food for six weeks.

Look!, she said
and pushed a biscuit
hard and brittle
to the side of her cheek
Crunch it up on the good side,
you've teeth on the right still
and little by little
Mother's pride shrank to
that tomboy wee girl on the
streets of Belfast.

I can, I will
danced defiance in her eyes.

I can climb a tree as good as them
I can run and kick a ball
kick a can I can
I will
I do it all
just the same.

In bewildered freeze-frame
on the day of discharge from under the
surgeon's knife
that left edge of my face swollen double
voice squeaking high-pitch gravel
like a tinker in trouble
that remaining row of teeth on the right
crunched down
began to bite.

Her eyes danced like November flames
unshakable confidence

28

mercurial imp of delight.
See! I knew.
I knew you'd do it alright.
Now, come on and eat your dinner
it's a beautiful day out there.

On Some Emerald Shore
For Mum

On some emerald shore
there is a girl
looking out over the ocean
her hands empty and open
her heart strong and pure.

What miracles her hands will perform
she is not yet sure...
the surge of life is primed in them
not knowing what lies before.

She does not yet know that her
hands will wipe away a thousand tears
that her heart
will weather a thousand fears
and that

that the wind out over the ocean
will slam windows and doors
and that the clamouring commotion
will send her to many unsures
to many not-knowings
many what-lies-befores.

She does not yet know
that her love will grow
three strong children
and that those empty, open hands
will wash many a floor.

Like us now, she does not know
that the rich bounty of empty unsure
will always be before her
as she looks out over the ocean.

On some emerald shore.

On This Day
For Heike Brewster

You look at us directly
from the window in our ribs
How is that possible?

that you are here
inside my chest and
also there
outside
as we stare
at the self-same life?

Well.
Feet planted
shoulder width apart
centre ready
down to
ground
arms scoop the heavens
as leaves might summon
light to fingers,
rain to roots.

light moving flesh bone
blood
hands and feet
woven here together
who could have known
we would meet
along the way?

Blessed relief
this gift you are
that you stand here
looking at us
on this day.

My Boy, My Boy
For James and Julliette

There he is
prodigious progeny
fruit of a thousand lives
here in the heat of Summer
silently stealing hearts with every breath
dismantling old ways with each gentle bat
of his newly minted eyelashes.

My boy, my boy
you're here at last
by way, perhaps
of some past stars
that made a pact to be so here
as you compact as lungs begun
we only know
that it was done
because look!
You are here
My Son.

and, of course, the days are wrought in fire
our hearts like rabbits caught in wire
thud more dreadful than before
(and they do, we don't know why)
but you have us so
and we have you
to love
protect
and hold.

You are so tiny
in my arms
and yet
here are a thousand people
lined up in the crease of your gown
dancing on a pin like angels
along the groove atop your frown.

We shall never be lost again,
my boy
only found in a foreign land

and yes
of course, we'll wonder why
the clouds grow dark in freedom's cry
and should you go (you shall not go)
for we will go
where you heed us to.

We thought you'd arrived at home
but it is us who have returned
to the start of life so new.

Look at you!
Tiny teacher
simple, suchling joy.

This freedom I wish
for you one day
may you gaze down
into astonished arms
and say,
there!
There you are:
my joy, our joy

My boy.

Oceans Together
For Caleb and Luce

What's an ocean anyway?

Waves of water that
carry me to you
ripples that tide us
back and forth
to and fro
not in knots
but rather

one complete movement from there to here.

Kinda swell
how that happened
on the rise and fall
of our breath as we hold dear life together
at the thought of it all.

There is no ocean that could keep us apart.

How could it?
We are waves forming
a part of the same sea.
I wave as me
you as thee
distinct together
both bound and free
around the world
we'll be, we'll be.

Shall we Ocean forever?

And Sea
we'll Sea.

Lionheart

Bright July Son
yawning into a broken world at
Portsmouth, 1947.

And at 11
brave soul
open hands
caned welt raw
by the war
growling on
in the bitter blood of
broken men.

Again and again
he got up
got on
began anew
Lion Sun
shining brighter than before at the
slings and arrows of
often-time
downright
for the love of God
bloody despicable
fortune.

And yet look
how the son beams
blatant defiance through his skin
atop the wide-eyed world
the kindness of his kin
roars victory
in the blazing hearth
of that
once
cold
harbour.

Evenweave

One stitch at a time
one step to go
always unravelling and
coming together
            without really knowing it
forever traveling
back to you.

I pull the thread
front side to back
I marvel at the
way it spreads
            this scene
from coherence to tangled dream
one side to the other
one town, one book, one pew
once me, once you
took one step and one stitch
            always unravelling
forever traveling on the spot.

But you know what?
Now I'm here
I look at the scene with just one view:
sitting here with you
the forecast is forever
and even leaving is only
weaving us closer together

one stitch at a time.

Five Lights

Light No.1
Diwali, New Moon, 4th November 2021

Night light

Incapable of holding on a moment longer
night falls around us
deadening dark carpet of
still-sudden thrum.

Here
we are together:
sparks in the stark of night
hearts ablaze
as one
continuous verse.

Light No.2
Bonfire Night, 5th November 2021

Explosions

Hot breath in cold air
cold hands in warm pockets
warm heart in dark night
dark light in fire rockets.

Turns out
burning bright
isn't all it was crackered up to be and yet
sometimes
the only thing to do
is put it all on the bonfire
eat a toffee apple and
let flames dance in your eyes.

Light No.3
Sierra Leone, 6th November 2021

Fire sleeks in street
i cannot write in flame but

if
i
did
tongues would scream
such horror
none could bare
to look or know
what it might mean

Light No.4
7th November 2021

Beacon

Darts into the driveway
through the open window
into the machinery
out of the speakers
bounces off the walls and
into my feet that will not stop
dancing to the beat
of light pulsing
in a vein
of leap in the
blood blood blood blood
thud of the night is alight
the cold white frozen concrete
won't let me go home.

Light No.5
8th November 2021

There is a light
It won't die
I try
to let it
but
kick or cry or fall or shout

it just
won't
go
out...

Autumn 1952
For Mum on her 70th birthday

Autumn 1952
when we began to fall through the
leaving of
one age to another
somehow through the passage
of a frown
down, down, down
the brow of my mother's mother's bough
the cradle full now with
you –

and across the water
the drink, the drink, the drink
in that there London Town
London Bridge is never falling down.

But here in the city
in Belfast City
the Road Falls every day doesn't
wait for Autumn, Spring, Summer
The Falls Road falls
every day a bitter Winter
shows the way
we pick it back up
tarmac it over
with some Mother's tears
kick cans in the street for sport
fold sheets, bake barnbrack, soda farls and potato bread
line the coffins of the dead
in the stomach of the living
then
put my brothers and sisters
as they put me
to bed.

Eight of us there
in the Winter of the Falls
cheeks and noses
red as roses

in the chill shrill air
rub your hands together
clap and stamp your feet
hop a scotch hot cuppa tea
hot chip butt
you'll see, you'll see
she is fearsome
she is pretty
she's my Ma
from Belfast City

I'll tell my Ma
when I go home
they pulled my hair
they stole my comb

I'll tell my Ma
when I get home
will I go home?
They stole my home.
They pulled my hair
I kicked their shins
I'll tell my Ma
about your sins.
I'll tell my Ma
I'll tell the Queen
I'll tell the King
about your sins.

Will I go home?
Where is my home?
I'll tell my Ma
I can't go home.

She is fearsome
she is pretty
she's my Ma
from Belfast City.

And, of course, it's September
and always morn
and over in that there London Town
the mourners come to see the crown

London Bridge
is falling down
see the kids round this old town,
my fair lady.

Remember it's September
and of course, it's the morn
on this day
every year
when you are born to us
again
dancing as the night becomes an age-old
brand new day.
Look how far you've come
we can hear you crying
that long way
away
even as you find a pearl
polished at the bottom of St George's Bay
as well-worn as hope is
for the way, way back.

She's been away now
for too many years
so, we sing all about it
bake bread with our tears
and raise fine childer
with a love that is strong
she takes her home with her
from the place she was born.

That's Belfast
you call to me
when I am far away
It's you I will be

Your Black Mountain
Cave Hill, City Hall
I carry them with me
I carry them all.

Fall from
Autumn 1952
to Autumn 2022

it is still – this September
we begin to fall through
the leaving of one age to another
somehow through
the passage of red, golden trees
the falling
leaves you where you stand.

70 years grand.

It's in the Trees
For Tony Green, on his birthday 23/05/2023

5pm I'll leave
or thereabouts
to see my friend again.

It's in the trees, he said
and so it was and sown it was
and although he did not know it
at the time
rescue
blossomed in his skin.
And so
to begin again
be born again was the gift that was given
that day.

Was it May? We do not know.
Maybe.
It's immaterial though
that light that grows the trees
that gift they gave
of rescue deep within.

Where he walks
and who he finds
may find it too
the gift of rescue that
dances between me and you
like air between the leaves
between the buses on the street
holding us as we move (and fall) and wake (and dream).

I really don't know what it means
but when you stop
the world
step off the beam
you'll know it
in the trees.

Christmas Bearings
For Raymond, on his birthday, 25th December 2022

He comes bearing gifts
in awkward boxes
tall, triangular
short and squat
confusing and surprising
it's a lot
to take in.

We're not ready yet
the stars are not in in place
the tree isn't up
the three wise men have not kept pace
and in case
you hadn't noticed
there's not even room enough in
here to swing a cat

But that
didn't stop you.
Still you came
bearing Battersea in your blood
and escape in your skin
slowly, year by year
you began to settle in.

We're not sure of this
the stars are out of joint
now you're here there's more than before
it's exciting and it's frightening
but what's the point?

Bear with it boy
you seem to say
year after year after year.
Look – the tree is up
the stars know their place
the table laid, the cups are filled
men wise and foolish all keep pace and
in case you hadn't noticed

you come bearing gifts;
your heart, your hands, your feet
beat out coordinates that guide you home
so come and take your seat.

Little White Petals

To all intents and purposes
it's an ordinary Saturday morning
in August

Sun shines,
breeze ruffles the tops of trees
a dog barks
neighbours are washing cars
kids skid about on bikes

All perfectly ordinary
except for the little white petals
on the window sill,
still, for what seems like an age
then dancing in the draft
leaping one might say
from over there
to here
upon this page

They have something to say to me
these little white petals
yet I can barely hear
The world is drenched in meaning
if you care to look
I think that's what they said

Why should curling white petals
have anything to say to me?
Or a pigeon or a rook?
What can they possibly teach me
that I cannot learn in a book?

It's okay to swoon
they say
it's okay to fall
it's okay to drink the moon
they say
it's okay crawl
to the next best thought

After all
we're only white petals
dancing on the sill
you're a god of love in motion
a chink of light that will spill
wherever you may walk
a spark of divine imagination that
on an ordinary Saturday morning
hears little white petals talk.

Resurrection in the Shower

every day
something goes away
and sometimes goes for good
or so it seems
until we remember
there was something infinitesimal
stitched into the fabric of the feelings we felt had died
and sometimes
on a spring morning
while listening to a song in the shower
we might feel the resurrection
as it all comes back to bloom
like an orchestra in our veins
defying doom to dare
stare us in the face
as we cry out in peels of light
reclaim our human title
and walk like beauty
through the minutes and the hours and the
days and the night.

Hope

She was so full of it
could hardly walk
waddling heavy with hope.

It didn't take long
for a man to grab her by the hair
drag her through the dirt
tear her skirt
and leave her for dead.

Looking up
eyes bloodshot and raw
she wondered what on God's Green Earth it was
she'd been hoping for.

Whatever it was
it wasn't here.

The Visitor

A man came last night
sat at the end of be bed
and said:

It's okay
there's no need to fear anymore
I can take it all away
I can remove the pain and longing
I can set you free
just close your eyes and rest, sweet child
you can come with me.

I sat bolt up
I glared at him
and seized him by the throat

Are you mad, I said
to take away
the pain of life from me
without it I would be quite dead
get out and go away!

I woke next morning
dull as gruel
a yearning in my gut
this pain will keep me warm tonight
will feed the fire's fuel.

What was he thinking?
Remove my pain?
Wipe the slate and make me plain?
Without it
art would surely die
I'd never write again.

So curled am I
with sorrows soft
and tears upon my cheek
So long as heart will beat with blood
I have these words to speak.

Did I Not Tell You?

Don't for one second imagine that you have suffered in vain
for every drop of rain
has made colours sing on violins
in choirs of wet grey stone
through trudging days in old English cities.

Just to your left side
walks a realm of heaven
in every inch
of rat-worn day
and craw crow cry
of charcoal smothered anguish.

I never left you
not once.

You left me.

and although
you go and go
here I am
in the margin of your melodrama
curling about the heavy pages
waiting to tip over
into a plain grey Saturday
when raindrops bring such riches

to say again
tread lightly, do not fear, do not lash out in terror stark
ye all are gods in this Kingdom here.

Romance Not Dead Yet

Alive and kicking off
moonlight from his sneakers
He walks in front of me
Always a few paces ahead
Of my heart beating in his
Ripped jeans and the melody
of him playing in my head
Like a song I've always known
Romance is not dead,
he said with a pen in his hand
And his hand on his thigh
as the moonlight spilled from his sneakers
and the sun rose in his eyes

Mostly Empty Space, Victorious!

sailing out against a sea of Virginia's Woolf's wading
helpless, harrowed sorrow
billowing skirts of jellyfish
yellowing and returning some hundred years later,
Victorious!
running rings round the Saturn edge of cups and saucers,
Victorious!
measuring out quiet desperation of coffee-morning moons,
Victorious!
and blue days on the backs of black dogs,
Victorious!
falling down in clumps of National Disgrace,
Victorious!
pricing out the seeds of springtime
for some dime-store demon-clown
goes *pop, pop, pop! culture war gonna get you*
on 5th Avenue,
Victorious!
I should have listened to my old man,
Victorious…
there's a field out back, beyond all this inglorious horse-shit
come meet me, come sit with me there, come lay by my side
there's no reason that I should still be standing,
Victorious!
the world is too successful to talk about
so kiss me,
Victorious!
on the memory
of Trafalgar steps
outside the gates of Heaven
in 1997
when we were last seen victorious.

By the Time You Read This
For Ken & Deni on your 35th Wedding Anniversary

It's only a matter of time
he says she says
on the edge of a flight
from there.

We can't do that, why would we?
How could we? Don't be ridiculous
is maybe how it went.

But none of that matters now
or then
as time has only ever been
waiting for us to finish our conversation,
that bottle of wine
and by the time you read this
we'll be on the next flight
right?

It's only a matter of time
before us
behind us
in which we've stopped
to do our thing.

Don't you see?
She says he says
there never were any clocks to stop
and in any case
don't you want another glass of wine?
There's still so much
to talk about.

Migrations
For Laurel

today is
in freefall

word on a wing

air thrilling
in dolls-house lungs and
ribs

breast filling
with such intense focus
sharp
beak
dive
deep

this will do
yes, this spot here
speck, hop, land, peck
ruffle, scuffle
nest.

Build, fashion, incubate
to gather in bundles
of remembering
of leaving and returning
in this conference of
connections.

Something shifts out West
tide, wind, probably the sun
who knows?
Something moves us anyway
it's time to go

Words fly in your fingers
away away hearts flutter
land leaving the flight path open
for seasons not yet invented.

Cry, Peace, Peace When There is No Peace

Sinead sings to me in the shower
like she did in New York City in 2008
when all I wanted to do was break apart on the page
by Bleecker Street, as if in some other version of myself
that wore a neat pullover slung with satchel
while the world went adulting to hell.

water flows over tired muscles
and tears make friends with steam
and she says:

I wanna make
something beautiful
for you
and from you
To show you
to show you
I adore you
Oh you

And your journey
towards me,
which I see
And I see
all you push through

I'm mad for you
and because of you
And I cry peace,
I cry peace when there is no peace
because there is no peace,
I cry.

I cry peace, I cry peace
BECAUSE there is no peace
BECAUSE there is no peace
and she tells me that you sang to her

(I know you did, I know she sang as you,
from you, for you, for *us*)
and she tells me that you sang:

They dress the wounds of my poor people
As though they're nothing
Saying, "Peace, peace"
when there is no peace
They dress the wounds of my poor people
As though they're nothing
Saying, "Peace, peace, peace"
when there is no peace,
days without number.
Now can a bride forget her jewels?
Or a maid her ornaments?
Yet, my people forgot me
Days without number,
days without number

And in their want
and in their want

who will dress their wounds?

Who will dress THEIR wounds?

And I cry
because there is no peace.
And I feel peace
because there is no peace
And I say peace
because there is no peace

And I will walk and eat and sleep
peace
until there is peace.

Over the Moon

I'm over the moon
honestly, I'm done
she only ever makes me croon
in stanzas giddy with doom
filling me up like a dreary balloon
pallid and pimpled, wet Wednesday grey
astonished wide face yearning to say
how inflated with dreams I am pregnant and full
pale bursting bright anguish tide-swayed we pull
out the plug and for 28 days out the words glug
like milky chianti spilling tears on the floor
or
stars in the gutter that glitter for just a bit more attention.

No
I tell you I'm done.
I've over the moon
gonna get me sun

gonna walk in the light
of a bright dawning day
skip beat tripping verses
in pavement cafes
riff Joni and Carole
strum Alan and Jack
with the sun in my sneakers and
the moon at my,

...at my

Ah....

Fuck it.
She's back.

Those With Ears and Feet

You have no earthly idea
how long I have been speaking with you.

My words are March winds that cut your face
back to the ancestry chalk of your tibia
a conversation that you could have kept preserved
in the vanishing squelch of boot in green-brown bog.

You don't remember the sonnet I wrote
in mist over fern, below swallows
or was it a flourish of pipistrelles
that you forgot to tuck into your breast pocket?
What was it? What was it?

You cannot see
and with no sonar
to alert you
the thickness of blind deafness
will divert you into the thrum
life support on dumb beep drum to
dot, dot, dot.

Listen. Can't you hear me?
I haven't gone anywhere yet
it is you who have dashed
the signal into white noise.

Those with ears and feet
have been coming here to meet me
every day
coming to hear me
write you poems in the
crackle of my pine-strewn floor
in the nearing of the shooting dash
of adder
subtracting
my sweet hazel dormouse
urgent eyed
they came and saw
not far, not far

they heard with hands and feet
not far, not far
conserving my opus in well-worn skin
eager to begin again tomorrow.

You do remember, don't you?

It was a nightjar.
A nightjar.

Tiger Night

Bolt of black silken sea
Come of wine or eggs or tea
Piercing fire bright
Cracker snap the dull night
Firecracker bright flight
Through the yellow net of the
Stout pot biscuit-tin town

Streaking through the streets alight
Tiger loose in night
Downs the dredge of grey daylight
Fire bright
Tiger flight

Bolt from black silken sea
See in me
The fire is free
Come for wine or eggs
or cake or tea
Come for light
Come for me

Sparkle star and crackle snap
The clenched rooms are
Folded back
Paper clips and pencil tips and
Polished glass and plates and cups
And cloth and cap are
Folded back and spread apart and
Tinkle tap the twinkle snap spilling
Into the street below
Like love tipped over

Over, over, like love tipped over
Like love tripped over the
Coal-black eyes in the
Billowing skirt of the ink-black skies and the
Proud prowl of the tiger cries
Teeth glistening in the clear cold sky
High, high
My oh my what a constellation of stars in the
Mouth, what a dazzling dance of luminous

Chaos in the stout pepper pot
Forget-me-not
Yellow-netted house

Round about and round about the
Sullen earth we shoot and shout and
Dance and spark, crackling and
Fizzing in the endless dark
Roundabout again begin
We bite the night and
Drink the stars dipped in gin

Bolt of black silken sea
Come for wine or eggs or tea
Bolt of black tiger night
Come again
Come for me

Saviour
for Chris M

Sometimes a saviour comes
not in beams at night
but in a garden bar on Brighton seafront
in broad May daylight.

And sometimes
a saviour brings not healing from on high
but cups of tea and ears that listen
so bravely
as you cry into the dark of a night
on an empty country lane
on the edge of a new year.

Sometimes a saviour
hears all the things you didn't say
but holds your hand anyway
as if you're the only person still alive.

Sometimes a saviour
cries out for your helpful heart
and says fuck it
let's get stark raving drunk
on a Wednesday afternoon
let's pretend it's 1922
and that I have just met you.

Sometimes a saviour
says come with me to New York City
I was the only boy there once
but you'll fit into the places
I go, I just know
by the way
your eyes peel the days away from the moon.

Sometimes a saviour
comes without fanfare
without cloak or wings or song
sometimes a saviour was there anyway
by your side in your life
all along.

Printed in Great Britain
by Amazon

44231997R00037